THE MAD LIBS

SILLY, HILARIOUSLY FUNNY, BELLY-BUSTING JOKE BOOK

by Stacy Wasserman

MAD LIBS
An imprint of Penguin Random House LLC, New York

First published in the United States of America by Mad Libs,
an imprint of Penguin Random House LLC, New York, 2024

Mad Libs format and text copyright © 2024 by Penguin Random House LLC

Concept created by Roger Price & Leonard Stern

Cover illustration by Scott Brooks

MAD LIBS and logo are registered trademarks of Penguin Random House LLC.

Visit us online at penguinrandomhouse.com.

Printed in the United States of America

ISBN 9780593658789
1 3 5 7 9 10 8 6 4 2
COMR

MAD LIBS®

INSTRUCTIONS

MAD LIBS® can be played by one, two, three, four, or forty players! In this book, you will find jokes containing blank spaces where words are left out.

Without reading the joke to the group, the READER asks the other PLAYERS to yell out words needed to fill in the blanks in the joke (NOUN, ADJECTIVE, VERB, etc.) and then writes the suggested words in the blank spaces provided.

Then, the READER reads the completed, completely original, and silly, hilariously funny, belly-busting MAD LIBS® joke to the group!

Don't forget to share the MAD LIBS® jokes with other friends and family to make them laugh, too!

- **EXAMPLE: (*Before and After*)**

Why do basketball players use a lot of napkins

when they _____ at the dinner table?
       VERB

Because they *dribble* all the time!

Why do basketball players use a lot of napkins

when they __*SLIP*__ at the dinner table?
       VERB

Because they *dribble* all the time!

QUICK REVIEW

In case you have forgotten what adjectives, adverbs, nouns, and verbs are, here is a quick review:

An **ADJECTIVE** describes something or somebody. *Lumpy, soft, ugly, messy,* and *short* are adjectives.

An **ADVERB** tells how something is done. It modifies a verb and usually ends in "ly." *Modestly, stupidly, greedily,* and *carefully* are adverbs.

A **NOUN** is the name of a person, place, or thing. *Sidewalk, umbrella, bridle, bathtub,* and *nose* are nouns.

A **VERB** is an action word. *Run, pitch, jump,* and *swim* are verbs. Put the verbs in past tense if the directions say **PAST TENSE**. *Ran, pitched, jumped,* and *swam* are verbs in the past tense.

When we ask for **A PLACE**, we mean any sort of place: a country or city (*Spain, Cleveland*) or a room (*bathroom, kitchen*).

An **EXCLAMATION** or **SILLY WORD** is any sort of funny sound, gasp, grunt, or outcry, like *Wow!, Ouch!, Whomp!, Ick!,* and *Gadzooks!*

When we ask for specific words, like a **NUMBER**, a **COLOR**, an **ANIMAL**, or a **PART OF THE BODY**, we mean a word that is one of those things, like *seven, blue, horse,* or *head*.

When we ask for a **PLURAL**, it means more than one. For example, *cat* pluralized is *cats*.

ANIMAL AMUSEMENTS

Why did the _____ cross the road?
ANIMAL

To get to the other _____ .
NOUN

Can a kangaroo jump higher

than a/an _____?
TYPE OF BUILDING

Of course they can!

_____ **can't jump.**
SAME TYPE OF BUILDING (PLURAL)

What did the dog say

when he sat on sandpaper?

" _____ ! **This is *ruff*.**"
SILLY WORD

What do you get

when you _____ a pig
VERB

with a giraffe?

Bacon and *legs*!

What kind of dog

can _____ time?
VERB

A *watch*-dog!

What did the cat say

when it bumped its _____ ?
PART OF THE BODY

"Me-*OWWWWW!*"

I asked my _____ ,
ANIMAL

"What's _____ minus _____ ?"
NUMBER SAME NUMBER

He said nothing.

What did one bat say to the other _____
ANIMAL

when it was feeling sad?

"*Hang* in there."

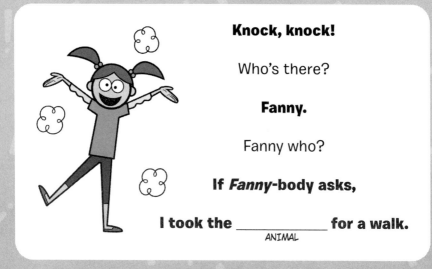

Knock, knock!

Who's there?

Fanny.

Fanny who?

If *Fanny*-body asks,

I took the _____ for a walk.
ANIMAL

What do you call a/an _____
OCCUPATION

who cleans a lion's sharp _____ ?
PART OF THE BODY (PLURAL)

Scared!

What do you call a polar

_____ in Hawaii?
ANIMAL

Lost!

Why do sharks _____ in salt water?

VERB

Because pepper water would make them sneeze.

Ah- _____ **!**

SILLY WORD

What kind of snake do you find

on a/an _____ ?

VEHICLE

A windshield *viper*!

Why are monkeys terrible

at _____ stories?

VERB ENDING IN "ING"

Because they only have one *tail*.

What smells better than it tastes?

A/An _____ 's nose!
ANIMAL

How do cows stay up-to-date on the news

and _____ events?
ADJECTIVE

They read the *moos*-paper.

Knock, knock!

Who's there?

Police.

Police who?

Police don't let your _____ _____
ANIMAL   VERB

on my rose bushes anymore!

What do you call the story

of "The _____ Little Pigs"?
NUMBER

A pig-*tail*.

Why do birds fly?

It's faster than _____.
VERB ENDING IN "ING"

What do you call an alligator that you hire

to find a missing _____?
NOUN

An investi-*gator*!

What did the duck say when she ordered a/an

_____ at (the) _____ ?
　　　NOUN　　　　　　　　　A PLACE

"Put that on my *bill*!"

What do you call a bear _____
　　　　　　　　　　　VERB ENDING IN "ING"

in the rain?

A *drizzly* bear.

Why didn't the _____ invite any
　　　　　　　ANIMAL

horses to its birthday party?

Because horses always say *neigh*

to everything.

What do you call a pig that never wants

to _____ anywhere?
        VERB

A *boar*.

What do you get when you mix

a/an _____ pie and a snake?
        TYPE OF FOOD

A *pie*-thon.

What did the _____ say
                ANIMAL

when she hugged the porcupine?

"Ouch!"

Why did the _____ little ducklings

ADJECTIVE

get grounded for a week?

They used *fowl* language.

SAY IT TEN TIMES FAST:

Little Lillian lets lazy lizards

_____ along the lily pads.

VERB THAT STARTS WITH "L"

What did the frog order

at the _____ -food restaurant?

ADJECTIVE

French *flies*!

Why did the _____ cross the road
ANIMAL

_____ times?
NUMBER

To prove it wasn't *chicken*.

What do you get from a/an _____ cow
ADJECTIVE

who always gets her way?

***Spoiled* milk!**

Why did everyone give the grizzly _____
COLOR

socks for its birthday?

It had *bear* feet!

What did the _____ squirrel say
ADJECTIVE

when its acorns got stolen?

"I've had a-*nut* of this!"

What did the _____ say
ANIMAL

to the rabbit on its birthday?

"*Hoppy* birthday to you!"

Where do _____ milkshakes
NOUN

come from?

Dancing cows.

What did the dalmatian say

after devouring its _____ at lunch?
                    TYPE OF FOOD

"Yum, that really hit the *spot*!"

Do ponies drink _____ ?
                  TYPE OF LIQUID

Actually, they prefer lemon-*neighed*.

What do you call a cow

who can't seem to _____ its way back
                   VERB

to (the) _____ ?
          A PLACE

***Udderly* lost.**

Why don't you see _____
ANIMAL (PLURAL)

hiding in trees?

Because they're very good at it!

What is black and white

and _____ all over?
COLOR

A zebra that fell in _____ paint.
SAME COLOR

How do bees _____ to school?
VERB

They ride the school *buzz*!

Why did the snake _____
VERB

the road?

To get to the _____
ADJECTIVE

sssssssssside!

Where do _____
ADJECTIVE

dragons go

when they retire?

To the hall of *flame!*

SIDESPLITTING SCHOOL JOKES

Why did the _____
ANIMAL

do so well in school?

Because she was

the teacher's *pet*!

Why did _____ cross
FIRST NAME

the playground?

To get to the other *slide*.

What did the _____ say
NOUN

to the pencil?

"You have a good *point*."

Knock, knock!

Who's there?

Weasel.

Weasel who?

***Wea-sel* be at (the) _____**
A PLACE

if you want to join us.

Why was the obtuse angle so _____
ADJECTIVE

and frustrated?

Because it's never *right*.

Why did the _____ bird
COLOR

go to the library?

To look for *book*-worms.

Why was the science teacher always

_____ and yelling?
VERB ENDING IN "ING"

He's a *mad* scientist.

Knock, knock!

Who's there?

Dewey.

Dewey who?

***Dew-ey* really have a test**

in _____ **class tomorrow?**

NOUN

Why did the cat have to _____

VERB

after school for detention?

He was a *cheat*-ah.

Why did the _____ get upset

NOUN

when her math teacher called her average?

It was a *mean* thing to say!

Where's the best place to _____
VERB

in your room when you're cold?

The corner—it's always ninety *degrees*!

Why did the homeroom

_____ wear sunglasses
OCCUPATION

in her _____ ?
A PLACE

Because all her students were so *bright*!

What time would it be

if a scary _____ came to school?
SOMETHING ALIVE

Time to run!

Why is _____ afraid
         NUMBER
of seven?

Because seven *ate* nine.

How did the porcupine beat the _____
                                ANIMAL

in the debate?

It had the most *points*.

What was the witch's

_____ subject in school?
ADJECTIVE

***Spell*-ing!**

Why did the zombie _____ home
             VERB
from school early?

He felt *rotten*!

What is _____ + 74 + 8 + 395 + _____ + 1?
         NUMBER   NUMBER

Too many.

Why did Professor _____ give the clock
PERSON YOU KNOW

_____ days of detention?
NUMBER

Because it tick-*tocks* too much in class.

What did the _____ say to the keyboard?
NOUN

"You're my *type!*"

What did the _____ say to the math book?
NOUN

"Wow, you've got a lot of *problems!*"

It took ten workers ten days

to build a/an _____ .
NOUN

How long would it take _____ workers
NUMBER

to build the same _____ ?
SAME NOUN

None—it was already built!

Who's the boss of all the school supplies

in the _____ ?
TYPE OF CONTAINER

The *ruler*!

Which _____ of the alphabet has
NOUN

the most water?

The *c*.

Why did the _____
ADJECTIVE

Gate Bridge get sent home

from school?

It got *suspended*.

What type of seeds do

_____ sharks like to eat?
ADJECTIVE

Human *beans*.

FUNNY ON WHEELS

What has _____ wheels and flies?
NUMBER

A garbage truck.

What do you call it when a dinosaur

crashes his _____ ?
VEHICLE

Tyrannosaurus *wrecks*.

Why do chicken *coupes* only have two doors?

If they had _____ doors,
NUMBER

they'd be chicken sedans!

Why did the frog take the bus?

Because his _____
VEHICLE

was *toad* away.

Knock, knock!

Who's there?

Canoe.

Canoe who?

***Can-oe* come out and _____?**
VERB

How did the ice cream sundae

get to (the) _____ ?
A PLACE

A fudge-*cycle*.

Why did _____ buy
PERSON YOU KNOW

the _____ car from the baby bird?
ADJECTIVE

Because it was *cheep, cheep, cheep*!

What do you do

if you see a spaceman?

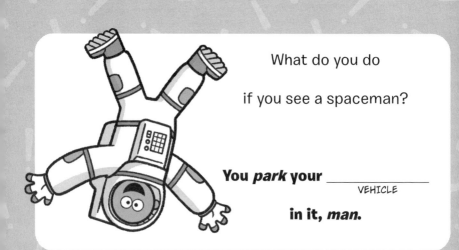

You *park* your _____
VEHICLE

in it, *man*.

How do you get a/an _____ to fly?
NOUN

Put it on an airplane.

Knock, knock!

Who's there?

Ken.

Ken who?

***Ken* you hurry up?!**

The airplane is about to _____ off.
VERB

What do you say to a frog

who needs a ride?

"Hey, _____ ! *Hop* on in!"
FIRST NAME

When is a/an _____
VEHICLE

not a/an _____ ?
SAME VEHICLE

When it *turns* into a driveway.

Knock, knock!

Who's there?

Carson.

Carson who?

Cars-on **the highway** _____ **really fast!**
VERB

What do you need

in order to _____ in Australia?
VERB

***Koala*-fications.**

What do you _____ when you mix
VERB

a car and a pet?

A *carpet*.

Why can't motorcycles _____
VERB

a flat tire?

Because they're *two-tired*.

Knock, knock!

Who's there?

Tank.

Tank who?

You're _____ **welcome!**
ADVERB

What is fast, _____,
ADJECTIVE

and crunchy?

A rocket *chip*.

Did you hear about the _____
SOMETHING ALIVE

who got run over by

the same bike every morning?

It was a vicious *cycle*.

What's wrong with making a/an

_____ out of an oak tree?
VEHICLE

It *wooden* go!

A guy walks into (the) _____ and asks,

A PLACE

"Who is the strongest _____ here?"

NOUN

A boy stands up and says,

" _____ is the strongest."

FIRST NAME

" _____," cries the man.

EXCLAMATION

"Can _____ come help me push

SAME FIRST NAME

my car to the mechanic?"

What did the _____ say

VEHICLE

to the tornado?

"Want to go for a *spin*?"

FANTASTICALLY FUNNY FOODS AND DRINKS

What's worse than finding a/an _____
SOMETHING ALIVE

in your _____ ?
TYPE OF FOOD

Finding two

_____
SAME SOMETHING ALIVE (PLURAL)

in your

_____ .
SAME TYPE OF FOOD

How do you keep your _____ sister
ADJECTIVE

from stealing your bagel?

Put some *lox* on it.

Knock, knock!

Who's there?

Olive.

Olive who?

Ol-ive _____
TYPE OF FOOD (PLURAL)

for dinner!

What did the _____ say
TYPE OF FOOD

to the banana when they

were looking for the _____ ?
NOUN

"Keep your _____ peeled."
PART OF THE BODY (PLURAL)

What did the skeleton say

to the waiter?

"I'll have a glass

of _____ **and a mop!"**
TYPE OF LIQUID

Knock, knock!

Who's there?

Duncan.

Duncan who?

Dunc-an _____ **in my** _____
PLURAL NOUN _TYPE OF LIQUID_

is my favorite snack!

What did the plate say when it went out for dinner?

"The _____ **is on me!"**
TYPE OF FOOD

What is the difference between

boogers and _____ ?
_____TYPE OF FOOD (PLURAL)_____

_____ **won't eat** _____ .
PERSON YOU KNOW   SAME TYPE OF FOOD (PLURAL)

Knock, knock!

Who's there?

Raymond.

Raymond who?

***Raymond* me to go to the store**

to get some more _____.
_____TYPE OF LIQUID

Why doesn't the _____ talk
_____TYPE OF FOOD

about becoming a pickle?

It was a *jarring* experience.

What did the _____ plate
ADJECTIVE

say to the grumpy plate?

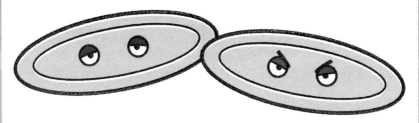

"Why do you have a *chip* on your shoulder?"

What did the _____ pie say
TYPE OF FOOD

to the fork and knife?

"You want a *piece* of me?!"

SAY IT TEN TIMES FAST:

Peter Piper picked a peck

of pickled _____ !
PLURAL NOUN THAT STARTS WITH "P"

Why did the poor, _____ baker
ADJECTIVE

buy a lot of yeast?

He was trying to make some *dough*.

Knock, knock!

Who's there?

Noah.

Noah who?

I *No-ah* place where we can get

_____ **fudge sundaes.**
ADJECTIVE

Why do restaurants catch

more colds in the morning?

Because of all the _____ *cough*-ee!
ADJECTIVE

Knock, knock!

Who's there?

Bess.

Bess who?

***Bess*-ides** _____,

TYPE OF FOOD

what do you want on your pizza?

What is the queen's favorite

_____ drink?

ADJECTIVE

Royal-*tea*.

Why did _____ spread peanut butter

PERSON YOU KNOW

on the road?

To go with the traffic *jam*!

A/An _____ walks into (the) _____
TYPE OF FOOD   A PLACE

and orders a sandwich.

The clerk says:

"Sorry, we don't serve food here."

Knock, knock!

Who's there?

Ives.

Ives who?

***Ives* been craving _____ for days!**
TYPE OF FOOD

What kind of _____ jokes
ADJECTIVE

do vegetables like?

***Corny* ones!**

What did the jam say to the peanut butter

when it got a new _____ ?
NOUN

"Don't be *jelly*!"

What did the _____ pickle say
ADJECTIVE

when the other pickle wouldn't stop

_____ about its problems?
VERB ENDING IN "ING"

"Just *dill* with it."

What did the _____ say to the knife?
NOUN

" _____ ! You're
EXCLAMATION

looking *sharp*!"

What's a potato's _____ animal?
ADJECTIVE

Alli-*tators.*

Why did _____ do aerobics
PERSON YOU KNOW

before drinking their juice?

Because the _____
TYPE OF CONTAINER

said to "*shake* well before

drinking."

What flavor _____ is never on time?
TYPE OF FOOD

Choco-*late.*

Why did the _____ blush?
TYPE OF FOOD

It saw the salad *dressing*.

Knock, knock!

Who's there?

Ada.

Ada who?

I *Ad-a* lot for dinner and now I'm really

_____.
ADJECTIVE

What do you call a/an _____
TYPE OF FOOD

disguised as a noodle?

An im-*pasta*.

Why do _____ peppers always win
         ADJECTIVE

archery competitions?

Because they

hab-an-ero!

What did the banana say

to the _____ ?
              ANIMAL

Nothing. Bananas can't talk.

Why did the _____ grape start crying?
                ADJECTIVE

Because his mom and dad

were in a *jam*.

What did the strawberry say

to its best friend?

"I'm *berry* happy

we are best _____!"
PLURAL NOUN

What did the tortilla chip say

when the _____ touched its cheese?
OCCUPATION

"Hey, that's *nacho* cheese!"

What did the doughnut do when its plans

went _____ wrong?
ADVERB

It just *rolled* with it.

Knock, _____ !
<u>VERB</u>

Who's there?

Bacon.

Bacon who?

I'm *bacon* you

a cake for

your birthday!

What did Charles Dickens say when he wrote

his recipe for _____ pie?
<u>TYPE OF FOOD</u>

"It was the best of *thymes*,

it was the worst of *thymes*."

HILARITY UNDER (AND OVER AND AROUND) THE SEA

SAY IT TEN TIMES FAST:

Six _____ snails
<small>ADJECTIVE THAT STARTS WITH "S"</small>

slid slowly seaward.

Who keeps the ocean _____ and clean?
<small>ADJECTIVE</small>

The mer-*maid*.

What do you say when the beach asks you

to _____ on it?
VERB

"Shore."

Knock, knock!

Who's there?

Whale.

Whale who?

**Whale, I guess I didn't make a/an _____
ADJECTIVE

impression the first time we met.**

What do you get if you _____ books
VERB

into the ocean?

A *title* wave.

What did _____ say
                PERSON YOU KNOW

when they ate the clown fish?

"This tastes *funny*."

Why are fish so bad at basketball?

They prefer to _____
                        VERB

away from the *net*.

Why did the clam give away its _____?
                                      VEHICLE

It prefers to travel by *shell*-icopter.

_____, _____!
VERB   VERB

Who's there?

Anemone.

Anemone who?

***An-emone* of yours is no friend of mine.**

Why doesn't _____ trust the ocean?
PERSON YOU KNOW

Because there's just something *fishy* about it.

Where does a/an _____ ship go
ADJECTIVE

when it's not feeling well?

To the *dock*-tor.

What happens when you throw your

_____ into the ocean?
ARTICLE OF CLOTHING

Try it and *sea* what happens!

What did the ocean say to the

_____ ?
SOMETHING ALIVE

Nothing. It just

waved.

SAY IT TEN TIMES FAST:

Selfish shellfish sell

_____ shells.
ADJECTIVE THAT STARTS WITH "S"

Why did the _____ mermaid scream?
ADJECTIVE

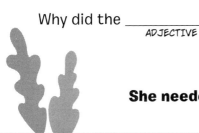

She needed *kelp*!

SAY IT TEN TIMES FAST:

Five _____ frogs fled
ADJECTIVE THAT STARTS WITH "F"

from fifty fierce fishes.

Knock, knock!

Who's there?

Beth.

Beth who?

Beth you didn't know that sharks

don't have _____ eyelids!
ADJECTIVE

Why did the _____ fish
COLOR
join the army?

Because it was good at driving a *tank*.

What do you call seagulls

that _____ in the bay?
VERB

Bagels.

Where do _____ crabs sleep?
COLOR

On the sea-*bed*.

What type of _____ only swims at night?
ANIMAL

A *star-* _____.
SAME ANIMAL

Why are mermaids so friendly

to _____ ?
PLURAL NOUN

They like to *wave*.

How do you make a/an _____ *float*?
ANIMAL

Mix it with root beer, ice cream,

and a cherry.

SILLY SPORTS AND HOBBIES

Why is Cinderella good

at _____ sports?

VERB ENDING IN "ING"

She always wants to go

to the *ball*.

Why was the weight lifter annoyed?

She had to _____

VERB

with *dumb*-bells.

Knock, knock!

Who's there?

Andy.

Andy who?

***And-y* shoots and he** _____ !

VERB ENDING IN "S"

What do sprinters eat

before a/an _____ ?

TYPE OF EVENT

Nothing. They *fast*!

Why did the golfer wear _____

NUMBER

pairs of _____ ?

ARTICLE OF CLOTHING (PLURAL)

In case she got a *hole in one*.

What type of _____
ADJECTIVE

sport can't be played barefoot?

Sock-er!

What's the hardest part

of skydiving with a/an _____?
NOUN

The ground!

Why did the referee call the police

at the _____-ball game?
NOUN

Someone stole third base!

Why are sports _____ always cold?

TYPE OF BUILDING (PLURAL)

Because they're full of *fans*.

Why can't basketball players _____

VERB

away on vacation?

They're not allowed to *travel*.

What do cakes and baseball teams

have in common?

They both need a/an _____

ADJECTIVE

batter.

What do race- _____ drivers
                          VEHICLE

eat for breakfast, lunch, and dinner?

Fast food.

What do you call a boomerang that

_____ away but won't come back?
VERB ENDING IN "S"

A stick.

Why are ice-skaters so good

at making _____ friends?
              ADJECTIVE

They know how to _____ *the ice*.
                            VERB

Knock, knock!

Who's there?

Water.

Water who?

***Wat-er* you doing** _____ **around**
VERB ENDING IN "ING"

asking me questions?

What is a cheerleader's favorite cereal

to _____ for breakfast?
VERB

***Cheer*-ios!**

Why did the ballerina quit the ballet

after _____ rehearsals?

NUMBER

It was all just *tutu* hard.

Knock, knock!

Who's there?

Moss.

Moss who?

Moss of my _____ time

ADJECTIVE

is hanging out in the park.

Why did the quarter get better grades than

the dime in _____ school?

ADJECTIVE

Because it had more *cents.*

What position

do ghosts _____ in soccer?
VERB

***Ghoul*-keeper.**

What's harder to catch

the faster you _____?
VERB

Your breath.

HA-HA-LARIOUS HUMANS

Why do we tell actors to

"Break a/an _____"?
PART OF THE BODY

Because every play has a *cast*.

Why did the old man _____ in a well?
VERB

Because he couldn't see that *well*.

What did the _____ say when
OCCUPATION

he jumped out of the storeroom?

"Supplies!"

Knock, knock!

Who's there?

Mule.

Mule who?

Mule **have to take my word for it—**

_____ **are delicious.**
TYPE OF FOOD (PLURAL)

When do astronauts

eat their _____ ?
TYPE OF FOOD (PLURAL)

At *launch* **time!**

Why did the thief wash his _____
ARTICLE OF CLOTHING

before he escaped?

He wanted to make a *clean* **getaway.**

What did the cowboy say when

he fell off his _____ ?
ANIMAL

"Help, I've fallen and I can't *giddy-up!*"

Knock, knock!

Who's there?

Doughnut.

Doughnut who?

***Dough-nut* think you can get away**

with being so _____.
ADJECTIVE

What did one tonsil say to the other?

"Put on your party _____.
ARTICLE OF CLOTHING

The doctor's taking us out tonight!"

I told my _____ that I broke my arm
OCCUPATION

in _____ places.
NUMBER

She told me to stop going to those places.

Why was the _____ good at falling asleep?
SOMETHING ALIVE

Because she could do it

with her _____ shut.
PART OF THE BODY (PLURAL)

How do you keep _____
PERSON YOU KNOW

in suspense?

I'll tell you later . . .

Knock, knock!

Who's there?

Butter.

Butter who?

***Butter* let me in.**

It's _____ out here.
                ADJECTIVE

What did the _____
                ARTICLE OF CLOTHING

say to the _____ ?
                PART OF THE BODY

"Don't worry. I've got you *covered*."

What happened when _____ stole
                        PERSON YOU KNOW

part of a calendar?

They got _____ months.
            NUMBER

How did the farmer fix his _____ ?
ARTICLE OF CLOTHING

With a strawberry *patch*.

Why did the lawyer show up

in (the) _____
A PLACE

in his _____ ?
ARTICLE OF CLOTHING

He forgot his *law*-suit.

Knock, knock!

Who's there?

Windy.

Windy who?

***Win-dy* you think you'll open the _____ ?**
NOUN

Why are magicians so good in school?

Because they're _____
ADJECTIVE

at *trick* questions.

Why was the politician out of breath?

He was _____ for office.
VERB ENDING IN "ING"

Knock, knock!

Who's there?

Joanna.

Joanna who?

Jo-anna come over and _____
VERB

a/an _____ ?
NOUN

What's the difference between

a well-dressed _____ on a unicycle
SOMETHING ALIVE

and a well-dressed _____
SAME SOMETHING ALIVE

on a bicycle?

A-ttire.

SAY IT TEN TIMES FAST:

_____ **the** _____
FIRST NAME THAT STARTS WITH "B"   ADJECTIVE THAT STARTS WITH "B"

bunny bobbled by the blueberry bush.

Why did the farmer's _____ leave
NOUN

to become a/an _____ ?
OCCUPATION

Because it wanted to go into a different *field*.

_____ , _____ !
VERB   VERB

Who's there?

Ash.

Ash who?

Ash-oo! Can I get a tissue?

What did one baby tell the other _____ baby?
ADJECTIVE

"If at first you don't succeed,

cry, cry again."

Why did _____ wear a helmet
PERSON YOU KNOW

at every meal?

They were on a _crash_ diet.

Why do spies like to read _____ books in bed?
ADJECTIVE

They like being *undercover*.

A cowboy arrives at (the) _____ on Saturday,
A PLACE

stays three days, and leaves on Friday.

How is that possible?

Friday was the name of his _____.
ANIMAL

SAY IT TEN TIMES FAST:

Four _____ friends fought
ADJECTIVE THAT STARTS WITH "F"

for the fan.

Knock, knock!

Who's there?

Ashley.

Ashley who?

Ashley, **never mind.**

I accidentally _____ **on the wrong door.**
VERB (PAST TENSE)

What did _____ say
PERSON YOU KNOW

when they walked into a/an _____ ?
NOUN

"Ouch!"

What can _____ keep
PERSON YOU KNOW

after they've given it away?

Their word.

JOKES ABOUT JOKES

Why did the _____
ANIMAL

cross the road?

To tell the chicken a joke.

Did you hear the joke

about the _____ fungus?
PART OF THE BODY

I don't think you'll like it,

but it might *grow on you*!

Knock, knock!

Who's there?

Icy.

Icy who?

I-cy _____ **!**
PERSON YOU KNOW

What do you call a duck

that loves _____ jokes?
VERB ENDING IN "ING"

A wise-*quacker*!

Why won't the _____ baker tell egg jokes?
ADJECTIVE

Because she's afraid to *crack* them up!

Why did the skeleton give up his career

as a/an _____ -up comedian?
              VERB

He lost his *funny* bone.

Why couldn't the

_____ -year-old go
   NUMBER

to the pirate movie?

It was rated *Arrrgh*!

Knock, knock!

Who's there?

Alda.

Alda who?

Alda _____ **here love my jokes!**
           SOMETHING ALIVE (PLURAL)

Knock, knock!

Who's there?

Meghan.

Meghan who?

Am I _Meghan_ you jealous

with all my _____-_____ jokes?
_{VERB}   _{SAME VERB}

When the tongue-twister champion got

arrested, what was the punishment?

They gave _____ a tough _sentence_!
_{PERSON YOU KNOW}

What do you call a/an _____ comedian
_{ADJECTIVE}

who can't sit down?

A _stand-up_ comedian!

Why are _____ dogs like cell phones?
ADJECTIVE

They have *collar* ID.

Why did the _____ have a hard time
ANIMAL

fooling the snake?

Because it's impossible to pull a snake's leg!

Knock, knock!

Who's there?

Boo.

Boo who?

Don't cry, it's only a/an _____ joke!
ADJECTIVE

Why did the scarecrow win a/an _____ prize?
ADJECTIVE

He was *outstanding* in his field.

Knock, knock!

Who's there?

Wendy.

Wendy who?

Wen-dy you think _____ will stop telling
PERSON YOU KNOW

all of these _____ knock-knock jokes?
ADJECTIVE

Where do thirsty comedians _____
VERB

at a party?

On the *punch line*!

IMAGINARY, MAGICAL, OUT-OF-THIS-WORLD GOOD FUN

What do you call a/an _____
_{ANIMAL}

with _____ _____,
_{NUMBER} _{PART OF THE BODY (PLURAL)}

a/an _____ tail, and _____ fur?
_{ADJECTIVE} _{COLOR}

Funny-looking.

Why did the teddy bear stop eating _____?
_{TYPE OF FOOD (PLURAL)}

He was *stuffed*!

What did the astronaut say when he

crash- _____ into the moon?
_{VERB (PAST TENSE)}

"I *Apollo*-gize."

What did President Lincoln say

to make peace between the spoons

and the knives?

"*Fork*-score and _____ years ago . . ."
NUMBER

How did the zombie hurt its

_____?
PART OF THE BODY

***Dead*-lifting.**

Why won't NASA _____
VERB

a duck into space?

Because the *bill* would be astronomical!

How did the tooth fairy repair her

broken _____ ?
PART OF THE BODY

With tooth-*paste*.

Knock, knock!

Who's there?

Gwen.

Gwen who?

***Gwen* do you think we'll send more**

_____ **to the moon?**
OCCUPATION (PLURAL)

How do you make a/an _____ umbrella stand?
ADJECTIVE

Take its chair away.

What does a skeleton use to call his friends

when he wants to

_____ with them?

VERB

The tele-*bone*.

Who helped the monster get ready

for the _____?

TYPE OF EVENT

Its *scary* godmother.

What's the best way to throw

a/an _____ on Saturn?
           TYPE OF EVENT

You *plan-et*.

How does the gingerbread _____
                                            NOUN

make his bed?

With a cookie *sheet*.

Why wouldn't the monster go to sleep

with the lights off?

He was afraid there were kids

_____ **in the closet.**
VERB ENDING IN "ING"

Did you hear about the new restaurant

that opened on the moon?

The _____ are really good,
TYPE OF FOOD (PLURAL)

but it has no atmosphere.

What do you call a fairy

that _____ really bad?
VERB ENDING IN "S"

Stinker-bell.

Why did the _____ cord
ADJECTIVE

get so annoyed with the metal wire?

Because it was getting

all *bent out of shape* over nothing.

Why couldn't the _____
OCCUPATION

book a hotel room on the moon?

Because it was *full*.

What does a/an _____ vampire
ADJECTIVE

write at the top of a letter?

"*Tomb* it may concern!"

Why was the elf

holding his _____
PART OF THE BODY

and crying?

He stubbed his mistle-*toe*.

What did the triceratops sit on

at the _____ ?
TYPE OF EVENT

Its tricera-*bottom*!

How do you _____ a story
VERB

to a giant?

Use *big* words.

Why did the skeleton quit working

as a/an _____ ?
OCCUPATION

His *heart* just wasn't in it.

Why didn't the ghost go

to the _____ ?
TYPE OF EVENT

Because he had no-*body* to go with.

What type of _____ dog
ADJECTIVE

does a magician have?

A *labracadabra*-dor.

Why did the moon stop eating

_____ for dinner?
TYPE OF FOOD (PLURAL)

It was too *full*.

What type of plates do

astronauts eat their meals off of?

_____ **saucers.**
VERB ENDING IN "ING"

What has three _____,
PART OF THE BODY (PLURAL)

_____ fur, sharp teeth,
COLOR

and three wheels?

A monster on a tricycle.

Where do people look for _____
PLURAL NOUN

that have gone missing in the Bermuda Triangle?

The lost and *not* found.

Why didn't the skeleton cross

the _____ ?
NOUN

He didn't have the *guts*.

Did you hear about the robot

who combined every book ever written

into one _____ novel?
ADJECTIVE

It's a *long* story.

LAUGHS HERE, THERE, EVERYWHERE!

Where do math teachers like

to _____ on vacation?
VERB

Times *Square*.

What type of drink do you get

while _____ on a camel?
VERB ENDING IN "ING"

***Camel*-mile tea.**

What's the best way to see

the _____ ruins in Peru?
ADJECTIVE

On the Machu *Picchu*-choo train.

Why was the road so angry?

Because _____ *crossed* it.
PERSON YOU KNOW

Knock, knock!

Who's there?

Wanda.

Wanda who?

Wan-da **take a/an** _____
NOUN

around the _____ **with me?**
NOUN

Knock, knock!

Who's there?

Wire.

Wire who?

Wi-re **you still** _____ **outside?**
VERB ENDING IN "ING"

What travels all around the _____
NOUN

by air, sea, and land but never leaves the corner?

A postage stamp.

Knock, knock!

Who's there?

Zoo.

Zoo who?

Zoo **you think we could stop**

for some _____ ?
TYPE OF FOOD (PLURAL)

What is the cheapest boat

a/an _____ can buy?
OCCUPATION

A *sale*-boat.

Knock, knock!

Who's there?

Camel.

Camel who?

I just *cam-el* the way

from _____ to see you!
COUNTRY

Knock, knock!

Who's there?

Crab.

Crab who?

***Crab* your _____ and hat!**
ARTICLE OF CLOTHING

What building in _____ has the most *stories*?
CITY

The library.

Where do elephants pack their _____
PLURAL NOUN

when they travel?

In their *trunks*.

Knock, knock!

Who's there?

Island.

Island who?

***Is-land* in _____
CITY

tomorrow morning.**

Why do time travelers eat so much

_____ ?
TYPE OF FOOD (PLURAL)

Because they like to go back for *seconds*.

Knock, knock!

Who's there?

Brett.

Brett who?

***Brett* you didn't know**

I would _____ the door!
VERB

Why did the chewing gum cross the road?

It was stuck on the _____ **'s foot.**
ANIMAL

Why do divers _____
VERB

backward out of their boats?

Because if they _____
SAME VERB

forward, they'd still be

in their boats!

Why do _____ love
SOMETHING ALIVE (PLURAL)

jokes about elevators?

Because they work on many *levels*!

Knock, knock!

Who's there?

Francis.

Francis who?

Franc-is **a country in (the)** _____.
                                        A PLACE

What city in _____ do pigs love the most?
                    COUNTRY

New *Pork* City!

Why did the _____
                    ADJECTIVE

airplane get sent

to jail?

It had a bad *altitude*.

NATURALLY FUNNY NATURE JOKES

What does a cloud wear

under its _____ ?
ARTICLE OF CLOTHING

Thunder-wear.

How did _____ feel
PERSON YOU KNOW

when they were struck by lightning?

Shocked!

What do trees wear to pool _____ ?
TYPE OF EVENT (PLURAL)

Their swimming _trunks._

What did the hurricane say

when it _____ over the town?
VERB (PAST TENSE)

"I've got my *eye* on you!"

Why did the cat _____ run away
ADVERB

from the tree?

It was a *dog*-wood.

_____ calls their dog
PERSON YOU KNOW

from the opposite side of the river.

The dog crosses the river without getting wet and

without using a bridge or _____ . How?
VEHICLE

The river was frozen.

Knock, knock!

Who's there?

Wayne.

Wayne who?

It's *Wayne*-ing cats and _____ **out here.**
ANIMAL (PLURAL)

If you drop a/an _____ _____
COLOR   ARTICLE OF CLOTHING

in the Red Sea, what does it become?

Wet.

I have lakes with no water, mountains with no stones,

and cities with no _____.
                    TYPE OF BUILDING (PLURAL)

What am I?

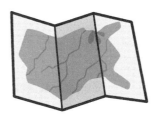

A map.

What did the tree do

when its _____ bank closed?
          ADJECTIVE

It started its own *branch*.

What kind of flower

_____ on your face?
VERB ENDING IN "S"

Tu-lips.

Why did the _____ think
PLURAL NOUN

the grass was dangerous?

Because it was full of *blades*.

What did the tree say when

_____ went to play baseball?
PERSON YOU KNOW

"I'm *rooting* for you."

Knock, knock!

Who's there?

Lettuce.

Lettuce who?

***Lett-uce* help you with your _____ .**
PLURAL NOUN

What did the _____ tree say
ADJECTIVE

to the _____ tree?
ADJECTIVE

"*Leaf* me alone!"

Why are pine trees bad

at sewing _____?
ARTICLE OF CLOTHING (PLURAL)

Because they drop their *needles.*

What kind of _____ do trees like to drink?
TYPE OF LIQUID

Root beer.

Why did the _____ plant light bulbs?
OCCUPATION

He wanted to grow a *power* plant.

Knock, knock!

Who's there?

Carrie.

Carrie who?

***Carrie* me.**

My _____ hurt
PART OF THE BODY (PLURAL)

so bad!

Knock, knock!

Who's there?

Manatee.

Manatee who?

Man-a-tee **would have been better than**

a/an _____ **today.**
ARTICLE OF CLOTHING

I stayed awake all night

_____
VERB ENDING IN "ING"

for the sun to rise . . .

Then it *dawned* on me!

Why do some trees _____ get into trouble?
ADVERB

Because they're kind of *shady*.

What did the _____ say
OCCUPATION

when he got stuck on an iceberg?

"I'm going with the *floe*!"

What did the flower say

to the baby flower?

" _____ **over, *bud*."**
VERB

What can run but never _____
VERB ENDING IN "S"

and has a bed but never sleeps?

A river.

Where do _____ trout keep their money?
COLOR

In the river-*bank*.

Knock, knock!

Who's there?

Cave.

Cave who?

***Cave* _____ a ride home.**
PERSON YOU KNOW

What happens when you throw a/an _____
COLOR

rock in the _____ sea?
LAST NAME

It sinks.

What is a cat's _____ dessert?
ADJECTIVE

Chocolate *mouse*.

I was wondering why

the _____ kept
NOUN

getting bigger.

Then it *hit* me.

How do you keep a bull from *charging*?

You _____ away its *credit card*!
VERB

Knock, knock!

Who's there?

Theodore.

Theodore who?

Theodore **wasn't open so I _____ !**
VERB (PAST TENSE)

What kind of tree can you

hold in your _____ ?
PART OF THE BODY

A *palm* tree.

Knock, knock!

Who's there?

Les.

Les who?

***Les* get someone to open the _____ !**
NOUN

When you lose your _____ ,
PLURAL NOUN

why are they always in the last place you look?

Because once you find them,

you stop looking.

What did one hat say

to the other?

"You _____ here.
_{VERB}

I'll go on *ahead.*"

What has two legs but can't _____?
_{VERB}

A pair of jeans.

What did the _____ -dollar bill say
_{NUMBER}

to the _____ -dollar bill?
_{NUMBER}

"You don't make any *cents.*"

What has *ears* but cannot _____ ?
VERB

A *corn*field.

What type of _____ pants does
COLOR

DNA like to wear?

Genes.

Why did the _____ cross the road?
SOMETHING ALIVE

Because the chicken was busy.

Knock, knock!

Who's there?

Irish.

Irish who?

***I-rish* you'd come out and** _____ **with me.**
VERB

Why did the computer keep

_____ and sneezing?
VERB ENDING IN "ING"

It had a *virus*.

Why did _____ throw the clock out
PERSON YOU KNOW

of the _____ ?
NOUN

To see time _____ .
VERB

What does every _____
NOUN

in (the) _____ get on
A PLACE

their birthday?

A year older.

What do you call the biggest moth

in (the) _____ ?
A PLACE

A *mam-moth.*

I'm light as a feather, but you can't hold me

for more than _____ minutes. What am I?
NUMBER

Your breath.

Knock, knock!

Who's there.

Avenue.

Avenue who?

***Aven-ue* ever heard of**

ringing the _____ -bell?
NOUN

What should you wear

to a tea _____ ?
TYPE OF EVENT

A *T*-shirt.

Knock, knock!

Who's there?

Patrick.

Patrick who?

Pa-tricked me into

_____ on this door.

VERB ENDING IN "ING"

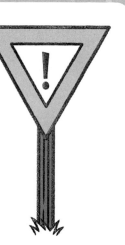

Where would you find a/an _____ ?

NOUN

The same place you lost it.

Why did the _____ go outside

OCCUPATION

with his piggy bank?

He wanted to see a *change* in the weather.

Knock, knock!

Who's there?

Hannah.

Hannah who?

Hann-ah **me that screwdriver**

so I can fix the _____ **!**
NOUN

What is _____ but not as heavy?
COLOR

Light _____ .
SAME COLOR

Why was the broom late

for the _____ ?
TYPE OF EVENT

It over-*swept*.

What tastes better than it _____ ?
VERB ENDING IN "S"

Your tongue.

What *runs* around a/an

_____ but never moves?
TYPE OF BUILDING

A fence.

Knock, knock!

Who's there?

Eileen.

Eileen who?

If *Ei-leen* over too far,

my cowboy _____ will fall off.
ARTICLE OF CLOTHING

What do you call a/an _____ dinosaur
ADJECTIVE

with bad eyesight?

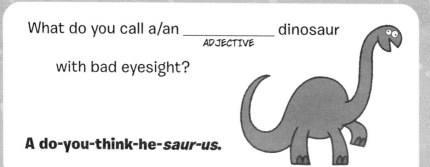

A do-you-think-he-*saur-us*.

I copy your every _____,
NOUN

but you can't catch me.

What am I?

Your shadow.

What has legs but can't

_____?
VERB

A table.

Why are fish so smart?

Because they _____ **in *schools*.**
VERB

Which is heavier:

a ton of _____ or
PLURAL NOUN

a ton of _____ ?
PLURAL NOUN

Neither—they both weigh a ton.

What did the _____ finger
ADJECTIVE

say to the thumb?

"I'm in *glove* with you!"

Knock, knock!

Who's there?

Orange.

Orange who?

***Orange* you _____ to see me?**
ADJECTIVE

How does a polite lion greet the other

animals in (the) _____ ?
A PLACE

"Pleased to *eat* you."

What do you call a/an _____
ADJECTIVE

dog with a fever?

A *hot* dog.

What is full of holes

but still holds _____?
TYPE OF LIQUID

A sponge.

What do you call two _____ bananas
ADJECTIVE

that someone left on the _____?
NOUN

A pair of *slip*-pers.